HAIL TO THE CHIEF!

FUN FACTS AND ACTIVITIES ABOUT THE US PRESIDENTS

REMEMBER THE LADIES!

BY TRACEY WEST

GROSSET & DUNLAP ★ An Imprint of Penguin Random House

CHECK OUT THESE WEBSITES IF YOU NEED HELP WITH ANY OF THE ACTIVITIES IN THIS BOOK.
AMERICANHISTORY.SI.EDU/PRESIDENCY
AMERICANHISTORY.SI.EDU/FIRST-LADIES/INTRODUCTION
WWW.WHITEHOUSE.GOV/1600/PRESIDENTS
WWW.WHITEHOUSE.GOV/1600/FIRST-LADIES

GROSSET & DUNLAP

Penguin Young Readers Group
An Imprint of Penguin Random House LLC

✳ Smithsonian

This trademark is owned by the Smithsonian Institution
and is registered in the U.S. Patent and Trademark Office.

Smithsonian Enterprises:
Christopher Liedel, President
Carol LeBlanc, Senior Vice President, Education and Consumer Products
Brigid Ferraro, Vice President, Education and Consumer Products
Ellen Nanney, Licensing Manager
Kealy Gordon, Product Development Manager

James G. Barber, Historian, Smithsonian National Portrait Gallery

CONTENTS

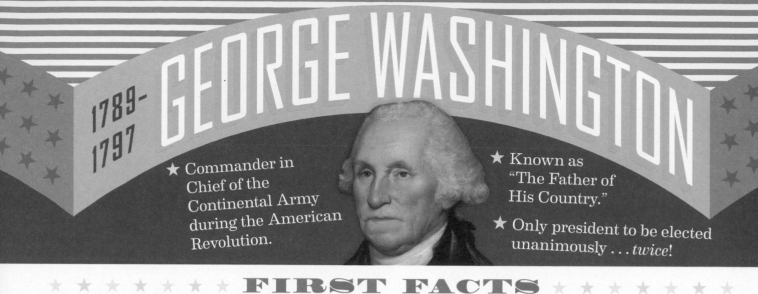

1789–1797 GEORGE WASHINGTON

★ Commander in Chief of the Continental Army during the American Revolution.

★ Known as "The Father of His Country."

★ Only president to be elected unanimously . . . *twice!*

★ ★ ★ ★ ★ ★ ★ FIRST FACTS ★ ★ ★ ★ ★ ★ ★

READ THE CLUES AND WRITE THE ANSWERS IN THIS CROSSWORD PUZZLE ABOUT THE FIRST PRESIDENT.

ACROSS

1 His wife's name was _____.

3 Like many men of his time, he wore a _____ on his head.

5 You can still visit his home, _____, on the banks of the Potomac River.

7 He was the first president to make this a national holiday.

8 He fought in the French and _____ War.

9 There is a famous story about him cutting down a _____ tree, but it's NOT TRUE!

DOWN

2 Washington was the only president to be unanimously elected _____.

4 Another story says he threw a silver _____ all the way across the Potomac. Also NOT TRUE! (Maybe another river, but not the Potomac: too wide!)

6 He was born in this state.

7 Washington had false _____, but they were not made of wood.

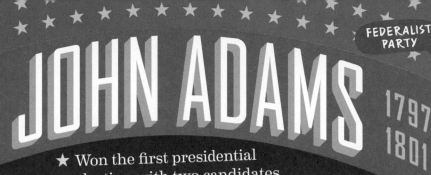

JOHN ADAMS

1797–1801

★ Won the first presidential election with two candidates. (The loser? Thomas Jefferson.)

★ First president to live in the White House.

★ Died on July 4, 1826, the same day as Jefferson—and 50 years after the Declaration of Independence.

★ ★ ★ ★ ★ ★ ★ **HAPPY BIRTHDAY!** ★ ★ ★ ★ ★

ALL ACROSS THE UNITED STATES, PEOPLE CELEBRATE JULY FOURTH WITH FANTASTIC FIREWORKS DISPLAYS. DRAW WHERE YOU LIVE AND ADD SOME FIREWORKS TO THE NIGHT SKY.

First Lady

ABIGAIL ADAMS

1797–1801

★ Loved reading books and discussing politics.   ★ Taught herself French.

★ Encouraged her husband to support education for young women.

★ Now famous for her hundreds of letters, which describe
life during and after the American Revolutionary War.

Dear Abigail

WRITE A LETTER TO ABIGAIL ADAMS. WHAT WOULD YOU LIKE TO KNOW ABOUT LIFE IN COLONIAL TIMES?

INK

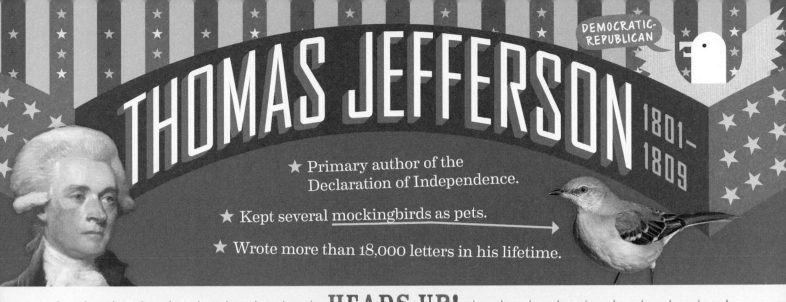

THOMAS JEFFERSON 1801–1809

★ Primary author of the Declaration of Independence.

★ Kept several mockingbirds as pets.

★ Wrote more than 18,000 letters in his lifetime.

★ ★ ★ ★ ★ ★ ★ ★ ★ ★ ★ **HEADS UP!** ★ ★ ★ ★ ★ ★ ★ ★ ★ ★ ★

THOMAS JEFFERSON IS ONE OF FOUR PRESIDENTS CARVED INTO MOUNT RUSHMORE IN SOUTH DAKOTA. WHO DO YOU THINK DESERVES TO BE ADDED TO THIS MONUMENTAL SCULPTURE? DRAW YOUR SCULPTURE.

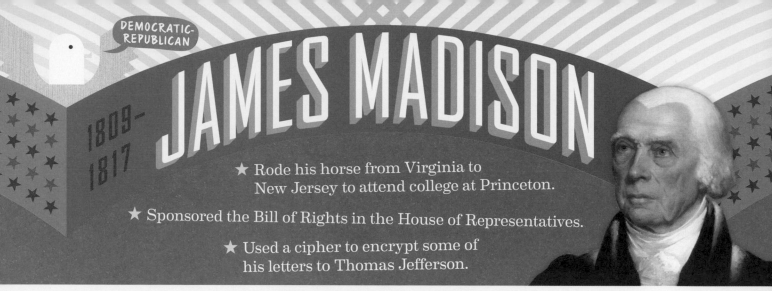

JAMES MADISON

1809–1817

★ Rode his horse from Virginia to New Jersey to attend college at Princeton.

★ Sponsored the Bill of Rights in the House of Representatives.

★ Used a cipher to encrypt some of his letters to Thomas Jefferson.

★ ★ ★ ★ ★ ★ ★ ★ ★ MADISON'S RIDE ★ ★ ★ ★ ★ ★ ★ ★ ★

HELP JAMES MADISON GET FROM HIS HOME IN MONTPELIER, VIRGINIA, TO COLLEGE IN PRINCETON, NEW JERSEY.

START!

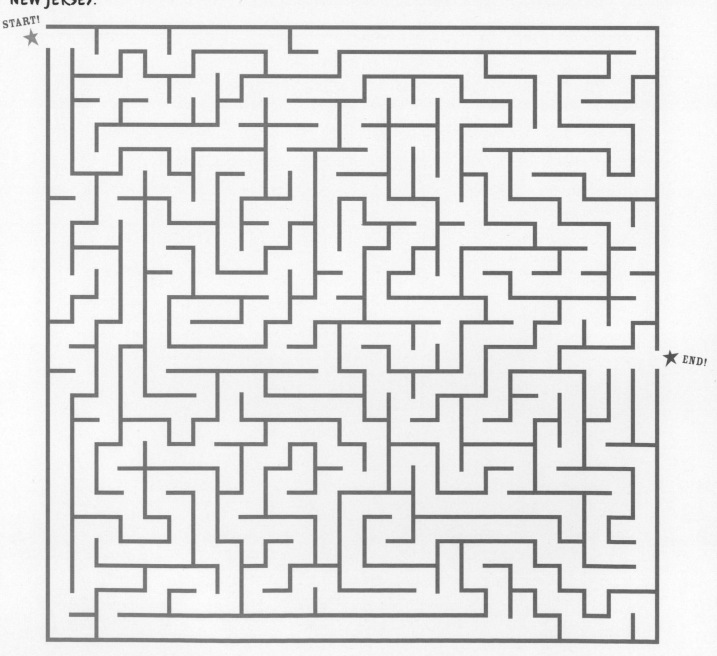

END!

First Lady
DOLLEY MADISON
1809–1817

★ Known as a gracious, savvy, and stylish host at the White House.

★ Helped make ice cream popular in the United States.

★ ★ ★ ★ ★ ★ ★ ★ SELL IT! ★ ★ ★ ★ ★ ★ ★ ★

DOLLEY MADISON'S FAVORITE FLAVOR OF ICE CREAM WAS—*OYSTER!* CREATE YOUR OWN ICE CREAM FLAVOR. ADD A LABEL AND SLOGAN TELLING PEOPLE WHY THEY SHOULD TRY IT.

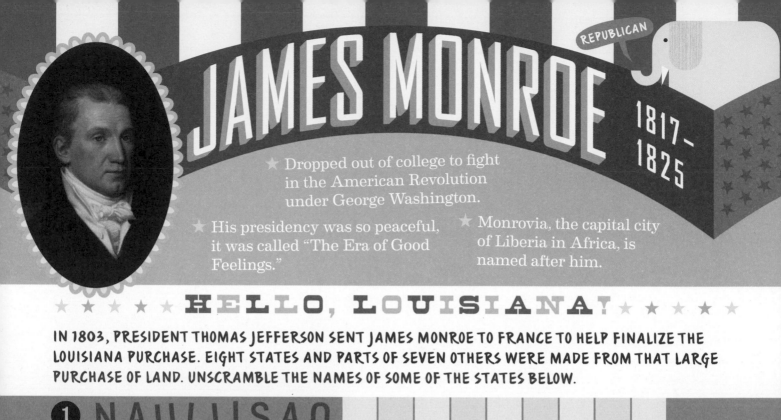

JAMES MONROE

REPUBLICAN

1817–1825

★ Dropped out of college to fight in the American Revolution under George Washington.

★ His presidency was so peaceful, it was called "The Era of Good Feelings."

★ Monrovia, the capital city of Liberia in Africa, is named after him.

★ ★ ★ ★ HELLO, LOUISIANA! ★ ★ ★ ★

IN 1803, PRESIDENT THOMAS JEFFERSON SENT JAMES MONROE TO FRANCE TO HELP FINALIZE THE LOUISIANA PURCHASE. EIGHT STATES AND PARTS OF SEVEN OTHERS WERE MADE FROM THAT LARGE PURCHASE OF LAND. UNSCRAMBLE THE NAMES OF SOME OF THE STATES BELOW.

1. NAULIISAO
2. SMOIRUSI
3. SKRANASA
4. AWOI
5. THORN AAKTDO
6. THOUS KODATA
7. SKBRANEA
8. AOMKOLAH
9. SNAKSA
10. ROADCOOL
11. GNOMIWY
12. ANTMANO
13. MOATSNENI

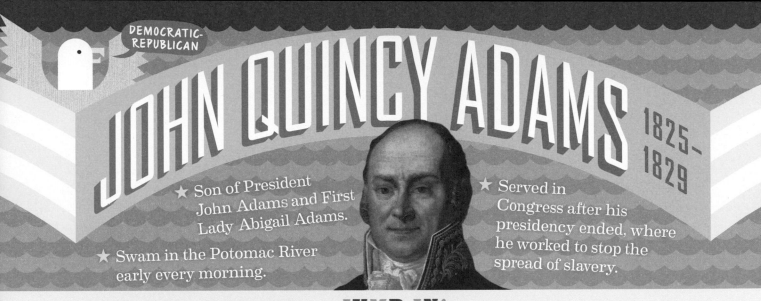

JOHN QUINCY ADAMS 1825–1829

★ Son of President John Adams and First Lady Abigail Adams.

★ Swam in the Potomac River early every morning.

★ Served in Congress after his presidency ended, where he worked to stop the spread of slavery.

★ ★ ★ ★ ★ ★ ★ ★ ★ ★ ★ ★ **JUMP IN!** ★ ★ ★ ★ ★ ★ ★ ★ ★ ★ ★ ★

DRAW YOURSELF SWIMMING IN THE POTOMAC RIVER NEAR WASHINGTON, DC, WITH JOHN QUINCY ADAMS.

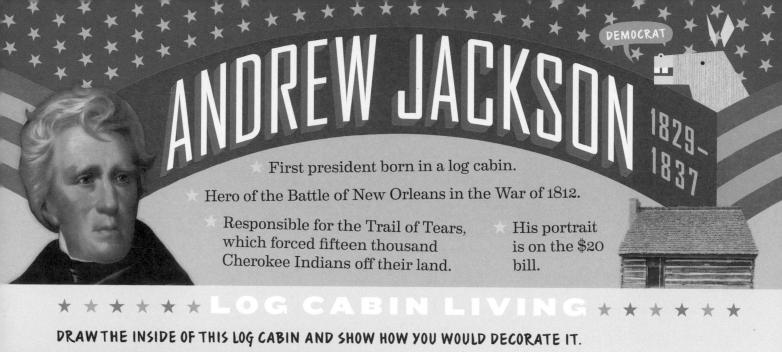

ANDREW JACKSON

DEMOCRAT

1829–1837

★ First president born in a log cabin.

★ Hero of the Battle of New Orleans in the War of 1812.

★ Responsible for the Trail of Tears, which forced fifteen thousand Cherokee Indians off their land.

★ His portrait is on the $20 bill.

★ ★ ★ ★ ★ ★ LOG CABIN LIVING ★ ★ ★ ★ ★ ★

DRAW THE INSIDE OF THIS LOG CABIN AND SHOW HOW YOU WOULD DECORATE IT.

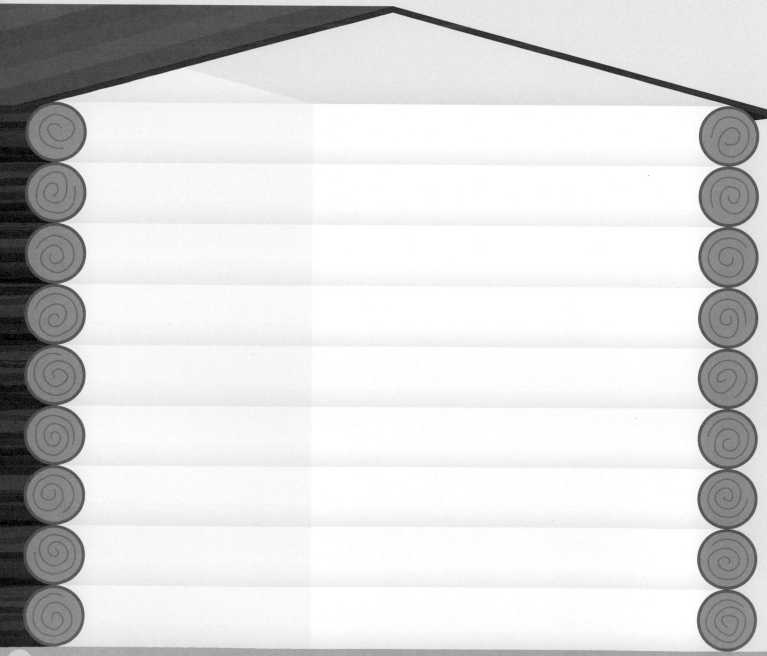

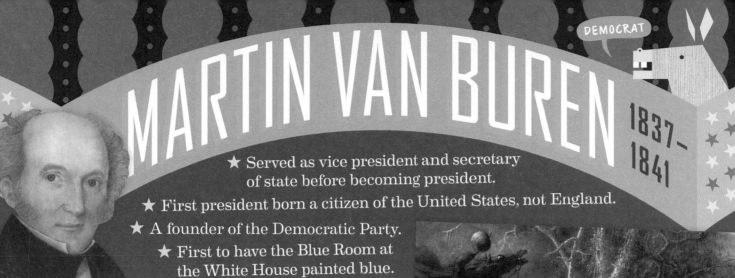

MARTIN VAN BUREN

DEMOCRAT

1837–1841

★ Served as vice president and secretary of state before becoming president.

★ First president born a citizen of the United States, not England.

★ A founder of the Democratic Party.

★ First to have the Blue Room at the White House painted blue.

★ ★ ★ ★ A WRITER OF LEGEND

VAN BUREN WAS FRIENDS WITH WASHINGTON IRVING, AUTHOR OF *THE LEGEND OF SLEEPY HOLLOW*. THIS FAMOUS SHORT STORY IS ABOUT THE HEADLESS GHOST OF A SOLDIER FROM THE AMERICAN REVOLUTION.

DRAW YOUR SCARIEST GHOST OR MONSTER HERE.

1841 WILLIAM HENRY HARRISON

★ Gave his two-hour inauguration speech in the cold with no coat.

★ Served only 32 days and then died of pneumonia.

★ As a US Army general, defeated the Shawnee leader Tecumseh, a British ally, in the War of 1812.

★ ★ ★ ★ ★ ★ GET ELECTED ★ ★ ★ ★ ★ ★ ★ ★

"TIPPECANOE AND TYLER TOO!" WAS HARRISON'S CATCHY CAMPAIGN SLOGAN. TIPPECANOE WAS A BATTLE HE HAD WON, AND JOHN TYLER WAS HIS VICE-PRESIDENTIAL CANDIDATE. WHAT OFFICE WOULD YOU RUN FOR? DRAW A CAMPAIGN POSTER. DON'T FORGET A SLOGAN!

JOHN TYLER

WHIG PARTY

1841–1845

★ Nicknamed "His Accidency" because he took office after Harrison died.

★ Holds the record for president with the most children: 15!

★ Later, supported the Southern states of the Confederacy.

★ TYLER'S TOTS ★ ★ ★ ★ ★ ★ ★

CAN YOU FIND THE NAMES OF TYLER'S 15 CHILDREN IN THE GRID BELOW? LOOK UP, DOWN, ACROSS, AND BACKWARD.

```
L  A  C  H  L  A  N  O  Y  L  L
E  N  N  A  L  I  L  T  J  O
J  O  H  N  L  L  M  D  O  N
M  R  L  H  L  U  A  D  H  T
A  P  E  C  E  J  R  I  N  T
L  E  T  H  W  L  Y  V  J  R
I  A  I  I  E  F  Y  A  R  E
C  R  C  O  Z  H  N  D  R  B
E  L  I  Z  A  B  E  T  H  O
T  Y  A  F  T  R  E  B  O  R
```

NAME BANK Alice Anne David Elizabeth John John Jr. Julia Lachlan
Leticia Lyon Mary Pearl Robert Robert F. Tazewell

15

First Kids

CAN YOU IMAGINE GROWING UP IN THE WHITE HOUSE? THE CHILDREN OF PRESIDENTS CAN! UNSCRAMBLE THE WORDS TO COMPLETE THESE FACTS ABOUT FIRST KIDS.

1 Harry Truman's daughter, Margaret, grew up to write popular STYYMER novels.

2 When she grew up, Caroline Kennedy became the US Ambassador to PAANJ.

3 Amy Carter played in a ETRE SHOUE in the White House backyard.

4 Abraham Lincoln's son Tad liked to pretend he was a DREISOL.

5 When she was 16, Malia Obama got a job as a production assistant on a VIEETOINLS show.

6 Teddy Roosevelt's daughter Ethel served as a RUNSE in World War I.

7 Ethel's brother Quentin was a THEFIGR pilot who died in the same war.

8 Franklin Roosevelt Jr. was elected to SGRCONES.

9 Gerald Ford's daughter, Susan, was the only first kid to have her RENOIS MORP in the White House.

10 Ron Reagan Jr. studied to be a LATLEB dancer.

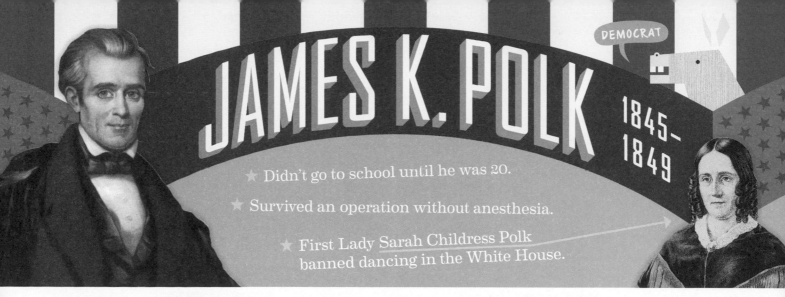

★ Didn't go to school until he was 20.

★ Survived an operation without anesthesia.

★ First Lady Sarah Childress Polk banned dancing in the White House.

★ ★ ★ ★ SCRAMBLED STATES ★ ★ ★ ★

THIRTEEN STATES WERE ADDED TO THE UNITED STATES OF AMERICA AS A RESULT OF POLK'S PRESIDENCY. CAN YOU UNSCRAMBLE THEM ALL?

1. WOIA
2. GROONE
3. STAXE
4. ACIANLRIOF
5. HAUT
6. COSSWINNI
7. NNOMAAT
8. THINNOSWAG
9. HOIDA
10. WEN OCIXEM
11. ROODCALO
12. ZIANORA
13. DAVENA

ZACHARY TAYLOR

1849–1850

★ Served in the army for 40 years.
Nickname: "Ol' Rough 'n' Ready."

★ On a very hot July 4, ate green apples and cherries, drank cold water and unpasteurized milk, fell ill and died a few days later, probably from some food microbe.

★ ★ ★ ★ ★ ★ SYMBOL OF PEACE ★ ★ ★ ★ ★ ★

THIS PEACE MEDAL WAS USED DURING ZACHARY TAYLOR'S PRESIDENCY. A PEACE MEDAL WAS A SYMBOL OF FRIENDSHIP BETWEEN THE US GOVERNMENT AND AN INDIAN TRIBE. DESIGN YOUR OWN PEACE MEDAL HERE. TO WHOM WOULD YOU GIVE IT?

TO

FOR

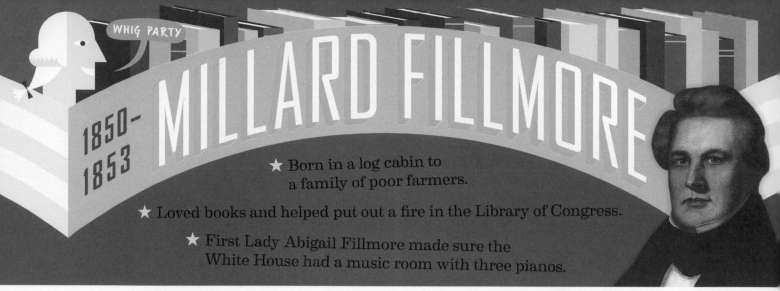

WHIG PARTY

MILLARD FILLMORE

1850–1853

★ Born in a log cabin to a family of poor farmers.

★ Loved books and helped put out a fire in the Library of Congress.

★ First Lady Abigail Fillmore made sure the White House had a music room with three pianos.

★ ★ ★ ★ ★ ★ **YOUR BOOKSHELF** ★ ★ ★ ★ ★ ★

TODAY THE LIBRARY OF CONGRESS HAS 838 MILES OF SHELVES! WHICH TITLES ARE ON YOUR BOOKSHELF?

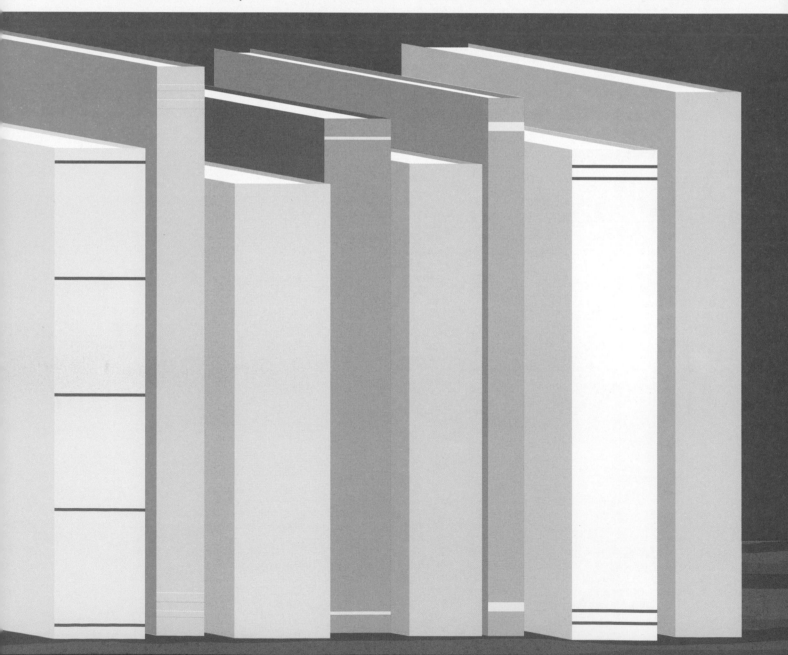

FRANKLIN PIERCE

1853–1857

★ Purchased more land to add to Arizona and New Mexico.

★ Friend of Nathaniel Hawthorne, author of *The Scarlet Letter*.

★ His father, Benjamin Pierce, was governor of New Hampshire.

★ ★ ★ ★ ★ RIDE ON! ★ ★ ★ ★ ★ ★ ★ ★ ★

PIERCE WAS AN OFFICER IN THE MEXICAN WAR. MILITARY OFFICERS WERE OFTEN PORTRAYED ON THEIR HORSES.

WHAT ANIMAL WOULD YOU LIKE TO BE SHOWN ON IN A PORTRAIT? DRAW YOURSELF ON IT.

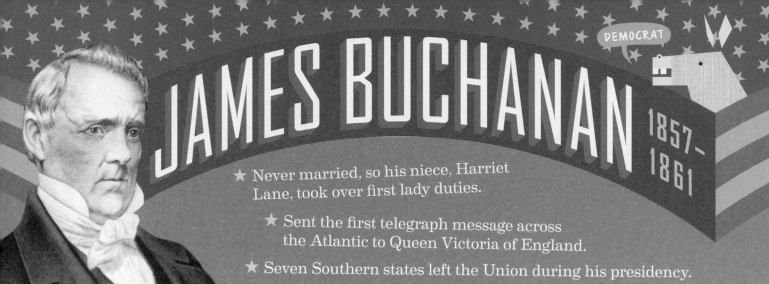

JAMES BUCHANAN

DEMOCRAT

1857–1861

★ Never married, so his niece, Harriet Lane, took over first lady duties.

★ Sent the first telegraph message across the Atlantic to Queen Victoria of England.

★ Seven Southern states left the Union during his presidency.

★ ★ ★ ★ ★ ★ ★ ★ ★ ★ **A NATION DIVIDED** ★ ★ ★ ★ ★ ★ ★ ★ ★ ★

IN ALL, 11 STATES SECEDED FROM THE UNION, LEADING UP TO THE CIVIL WAR. CAN YOU FILL IN THE MAP WITH THE NAMES OF THESE STATES?

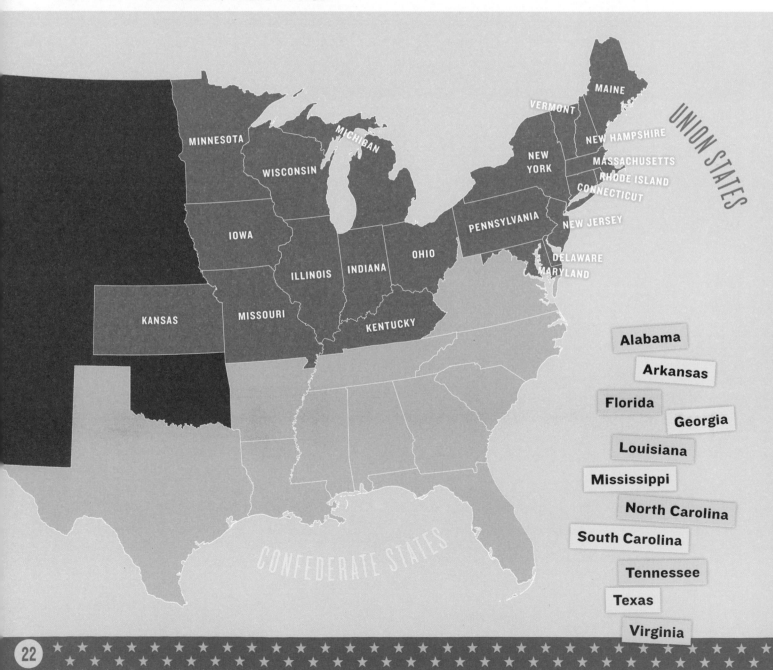

UNION STATES

MAINE
VERMONT
NEW HAMPSHIRE
MINNESOTA
MICHIGAN
WISCONSIN
NEW YORK
MASSACHUSETTS
RHODE ISLAND
CONNECTICUT
IOWA
PENNSYLVANIA
NEW JERSEY
OHIO
DELAWARE
MARYLAND
ILLINOIS
INDIANA
KANSAS
MISSOURI
KENTUCKY

Alabama
Arkansas
Florida
Georgia
Louisiana
Mississippi
North Carolina
South Carolina
Tennessee
Texas
Virginia

CONFEDERATE STATES

WHO IS THE MOST Popular President?

AMERICANS ARE OFTEN POLLED ON WHO IS THEIR FAVORITE PRESIDENT, ESPECIALLY IN ELECTION YEARS. ABRAHAM LINCOLN USUALLY TAKES THE TOP SPOT.

POLL YOUR FRIENDS AND FAMILY. WHO DO THEY THINK WAS THE BEST PRESIDENT? WRITE YOUR RESULTS HERE.

President	Number of Votes	President	Number of Votes
1 George Washington		23 Benjamin Harrison	
2 John Adams		25 William McKinley	
3 Thomas Jefferson		26 Theodore Roosevelt	
4 James Madison		27 William H. Taft	
5 James Monroe		28 Woodrow Wilson	
6 John Quincy Adams		29 Warren G. Harding	
7 Andrew Jackson		30 Calvin Coolidge	
8 Martin Van Buren		31 Herbert Hoover	
9 William Henry Harrison		32 Franklin D. Roosevelt	
10 John Tyler		33 Harry S Truman	
11 James K. Polk		34 Dwight D. Eisenhower	
12 Zachary Taylor		35 John F. Kennedy	
13 Millard Fillmore		36 Lyndon B. Johnson	
14 Franklin Pierce		37 Richard M. Nixon	
15 James Buchanan		38 Gerald R. Ford	
16 Abraham Lincoln		39 Jimmy Carter	
17 Andrew Johnson		40 Ronald Reagan	
18 Ulysses S. Grant		41 George H. W. Bush	
19 Rutherford B. Hayes		42 William J. Clinton	
20 James Garfield		43 George W. Bush	
21 Chester A. Arthur		44 Barack Obama	
22 and 24 Grover Cleveland		45 ???	

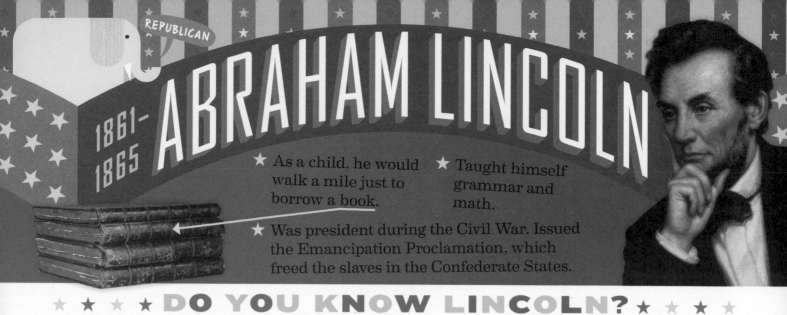

ABRAHAM LINCOLN

1861–1865

★ As a child, he would walk a mile just to borrow a book.

★ Taught himself grammar and math.

★ Was president during the Civil War. Issued the Emancipation Proclamation, which freed the slaves in the Confederate States.

★ ★ ★ ★ DO YOU KNOW LINCOLN? ★ ★ ★ ★ ★

FILL IN THE CROSSWORD PUZZLE WITH THE ANSWERS TO THESE FACTS ABOUT ABRAHAM LINCOLN.

ACROSS

2 Lincoln had a pet _____ named Tabby.

4 Lincoln is in the national hall of fame for this sport.

6 Lincoln was the first president to have this kind of facial hair.

7 Lincoln was born on the frontier in this state.

DOWN

1 Before he became a politician, Lincoln worked as a _____.

3 At 6'4", he holds the record for being the _____ president.

5 His wife's name was _____ Todd Lincoln.

ANDREW JOHNSON

1865– 1869

★ Taught himself to read. His wife, Eliza, helped him learn math.

★ First president to be impeached by the House of Representatives. (The Senate voted not to remove him from office.)

★ Alaska was purchased for $7 million during his presidency.

ALASKAN WILDLIFE ★ ★ ★ ★ ★ ★ ★ ★

MANY PEOPLE THOUGHT IT WAS A BAD IDEA TO BUY LAND SO FAR NORTH. THE PRESS CALLED ALASKA JOHNSON'S "POLAR BEAR GARDEN." TODAY WE KNOW THAT ALASKA IS RICH IN NATURAL RESOURCES AND WILDLIFE. CIRCLE THE ALASKAN ANIMALS HIDDEN IN THE PUZZLE BELOW. LOOK UP, DOWN, ACROSS, DIAGONALLY, AND BACKWARD.

```
M  U  S  K  O  X  A  L  P  A  S
S  O  X  K  W  H  A  L  E  A  A
A  B  O  L  A  A  S  E  E  X  P
L  I  F  S  K  R  A  L  H  O  O
M  R  D  A  E  B  T  G  S  F  L
O  A  E  L  A  O  S  A  L  C  A
N  C  R  K  M  R  L  E  L  I  R
A  A  L  R  A  S  Y  D  A  T  B
G  O  A  T  S  E  N  L  D  C  E
K  M  I  N  K  A  X  A  A  R  A
G  R  I  Z  Z  L  Y  B  E  A  R
```

WORD BANK

arctic fox   bald eagle   caribou   Dall sheep   goat   grizzly bear   harbor seal

lynx   marmot   mink   moose   muskox   polar bear   red fox   salmon   whale

ULYSSES S. GRANT

REPUBLICAN

1869–1877

★ His real name was Hiram Ulysses Grant. The "S" was a mistake that stuck.

★ Commanded the Union armies in the Civil War.

★ Friends with author Mark Twain, who published Grant's best-selling memoir.

★ ★ ★ ★ ★ ★ ★ ★ ★ ★ ★ **THIS IS YOUR LIFE** ★ ★ ★ ★ ★ ★ ★ ★ ★ ★ ★

ULYSSES S. GRANT FINISHED HIS MEMOIRS JUST BEFORE HE DIED. WHAT WOULD BE IN *YOUR* MEMOIRS? WRITE DOWN YOUR MOST IMPORTANT MEMORIES HERE.

RUTHERFORD B HAYES 1877–1881

★ Fought with the Union army. His wife, Lucy, cared for wounded soldiers.

★ As president, withdrew the last federal troops from the Southern states.

★ Had the first telephone installed in the White House.

★ AMAZING INVENTIONS ★

THE LATE 1800S SAW THE INVENTION OF MANY ITEMS THAT CHANGED THE WORLD—AND THAT WE STILL USE TODAY. USE THE CLUES TO HELP YOU UNSCRAMBLE THEM.

1873 Levi Strauss & Co invented these tough work pants.

UBEL SNAJE

1879 Thomas Edison invented one that could burn for 1,500 hours.

GLITHLUBB

1891 You don't need stairs if you use this invention.

ROTALACSE

1876 Alexander Graham Bell's invention made communicating much easier.

HEETLNOPE

1882 This mechanical marvel was one cool invention.

CREELTIC ANF

1892 This year saw the first gas-powered one.

BLIEMOOTAU

1877 This invention could record and play sounds.

GOONHPHARP

1884 You could say this fast-moving invention is amusing.

LEROLR SCORETA

1893 Makes getting your clothes on and off much easier.

PRIZEP

JAMES GARFIELD

1881

★ Wanted to become a sailor when he was a kid.

★ Rags-to-riches biography written for him by popular author Horatio Alger helped him get elected.

★ Shot after serving only 4 months in office; died 80 days later.

★ ★ ★ ★ ★ BEFORE PHOTOS

BEFORE PHOTOGRAPHY BECAME POPULAR, NEWSPAPERS WERE FILLED WITH ILLUSTRATIONS OF IMPORTANT EVENTS. USE THIS SPACE TO DRAW A PICTURE OF A BIG NEWS STORY HAPPENING IN THE WORLD NOW.

REPUBLICAN

CHESTER A. ARTHUR

1881–1885

★ Redecorated the White House because he thought it was too gloomy.

★ As a lawyer, he won a case for an African American woman forced off a whites-only streetcar.

★ ★ ★ ★ ★ **REPAINT THE WHITE HOUSE**

THE INSIDE OF THE WHITE HOUSE HAS CHANGED OVER THE YEARS AS PRESIDENTS AND FIRST LADIES REDO THE DÉCOR. HOW WOULD YOU DECORATE A ROOM IN THE WHITE HOUSE?
DRAW IT HERE.

DEMOCRAT

GROVER CLEVELAND

1885–1889
1893–1897

★ Only president to serve one term, lose the next election, and then serve another term.

★ Had a reputation for cleaning up corrupt government.

★ Only president to get married while in the White House.

LADY LIBERTY

PRESIDENT CLEVELAND ATTENDED THE DEDICATION OF THE STATUE OF LIBERTY ON OCTOBER 28, 1886. WHEN IT WAS FIRST MADE, THE STATUE WAS THE COLOR OF GLEAMING COPPER. THAT METAL HAS TURNED GREEN OVER TIME.

COLOR THE STATUE OF LIBERTY IN THE COLOR OF YOUR CHOICE.

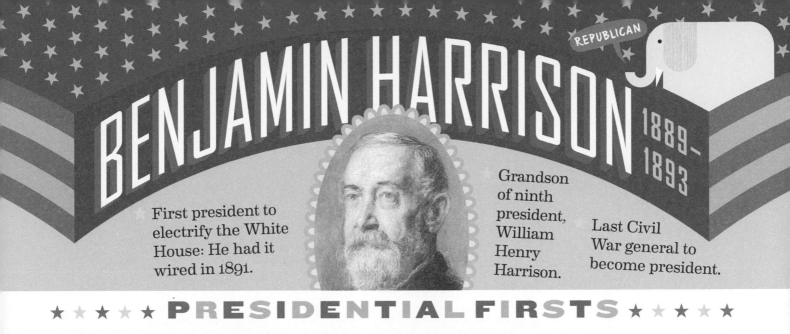

REPUBLICAN

First president to electrify the White House: He had it wired in 1891.

Grandson of ninth president, William Henry Harrison.

Last Civil War general to become president.

★ ★ ★ ★ PRESIDENTIAL FIRSTS ★ ★ ★ ★

USE THE CLUES TO FILL IN THIS CROSSWORD PUZZLE ABOUT PRESIDENTIAL FIRSTS. THE ANSWERS CAN ALL BE FOUND IN THIS BOOK!

ACROSS

1 John _____ was the first president to live in the White House.

4 The first African American president.

5 John Quincy Adams was the first elected president to be the _____ of a former president.

7 Rutherford B. Hayes made the first call on a _____ from the White House.

8 Calvin Coolidge put up the first White House Christmas _____.

10 Ronald Reagan was the first president who held this job.

DOWN

2 Richard Nixon and John F. Kennedy appeared in the first one of these on TV.

3 Martin Van Buren was the first president to be _____ a citizen of the USA.

6 Harry Truman gave the first presidential _____ on TV.

9 Andrew Jackson was the first president born in a _____ cabin.

31

WILLIAM McKINLEY

1897–1901

★ His picture is on the $500 bill.

★ Led the United States into the Spanish-American War.

★ Was shot and killed in 1901,
the first year of his second term.

★ ★ ★ ★ ★ FILL IN THE FLAGS ★ ★ ★ ★ ★

PUERTO RICO

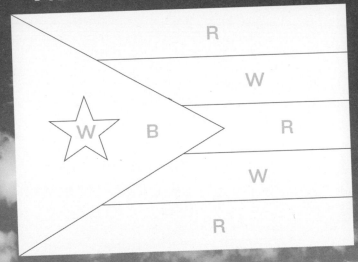

AS A RESULT OF THE SPANISH-AMERICAN WAR,
PUERTO RICO, GUAM, AND THE PHILIPPINES
BECAME TERRITORIES OF THE UNITED STATES.
(TODAY, THE PHILIPPINES IS AN INDEPENDENT
NATION.) USE THE KEY TO COLOR IN THEIR FLAGS.

PHILIPPINES

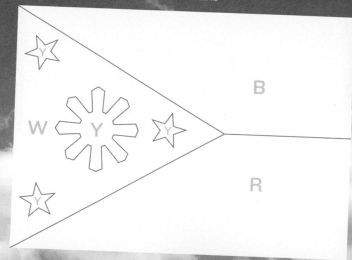

B = BLUE	R = RED	
BR = BROWN	W = WHITE	
G = GREEN	Y = YELLOW	

GUAM

32

THEODORE ROOSEVELT

1901–1909

★ Inspired the stuffed toy "teddy bear" after Roosevelt refused to shoot a bear on a hunting trip.

★ Created the US Forest Service to protect wildlife and public lands.

★ ★ ★ ★ ANIMALS IN DANGER ★

TODAY, THE US FISH AND WILDLIFE SERVICE TRACKS AND PROTECTS WILDLIFE. CIRCLE THE NAMES OF THESE ENDANGERED OR THREATENED AMERICAN ANIMALS THAT YOU FIND IN THE PUZZLE. LOOK UP, DOWN, ACROSS, BACKWARD, AND DIAGONALLY.

```
A  T  E  L  T  R  U  T  A  E  S
R  C  R  O  C  O  D  I  L  E  L
R  E  E  K  E  K  A  E  D  T  A
O  L  B  L  U  E  W  H  A  L  E
Y  T  J  A  G  U  A  R  D  Y  S
O  R  E  E  D  Y  E  K  R  O  D
T  U  O  S  E  C  V  E  L  T  E
O  T  E  G  I  A  Y  B  A  T  G
A  G  G  R  A  Y  W  O  L  F  N
D  O  A  N  I  M  A  L  T  T  I
E  B  A  L  L  I  G  A  T  O  R
```

WORD BANK akekee   alligator   arroyo toad   blue whale   bog turtle   crocodile
gray wolf   jaguar   Key deer   rice rat   ringed seal   sea turtle

WILLIAM H. TAFT

1909–1913

★ Only president to also serve as chief justice of the Supreme Court.

★ Started the presidential tradition of tossing out the first pitch at the start of baseball season.

★ The famous Japanese cherry trees in Washington, DC, were planted at the direction of First Lady Nellie Taft.

WASHINGTON, D.C.

★ BLOOMING ★ CAPITAL ★

THANKS TO NELLIE TAFT, VISITORS FLOCK TO WASHINGTON, DC, EACH SPRING TO SEE THE CHERRY BLOSSOMS BLOOM.

SEND THIS POSTCARD TO A FRIEND AND DESCRIBE WHAT YOU MIGHT SEE IN DC AT BLOSSOM TIME.

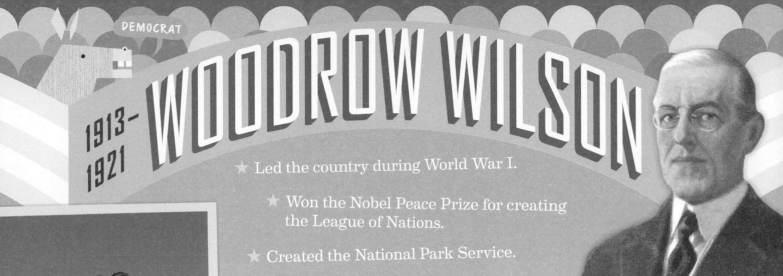

DEMOCRAT

WOODROW WILSON

1913–1921

★ Led the country during World War I.

★ Won the Nobel Peace Prize for creating the League of Nations.

★ Created the National Park Service.

THE NATIONAL PARKS
PRESERVE WILD LIFE

★ VISIT THE PARKS! ★ ★ ★ ★ ★ ★ ★ ★ ★

EACH YEAR, ALMOST 293 MILLION PEOPLE VISIT THE US NATIONAL PARKS. THERE IS AT LEAST ONE IN EVERY STATE; THE PARKS COVER 84 MILLION ACRES AND INCLUDE HISTORIC SITES, NATURE TRAILS, SEASHORES, AND MORE.

MAKE A POSTER ENCOURAGING PEOPLE TO VISIT A NATIONAL PARK THIS YEAR.

First Lady
EDITH WILSON

1913–1921

★ Was a descendant of Pocahontas.

★ Liked to drive around Washington, DC, in her electric car.

★ Acted as "secret president" after her husband, Woodrow Wilson, suffered a stroke.

★ ★ ★ ★ ★ ★ ★ GOOD GRAZING ★ ★ ★ ★ ★ ★ ★ ★

DURING WORLD WAR I, EDITH HAD A FLOCK OF SHEEP BROUGHT TO THE WHITE HOUSE LAWN TO GRAZE. THE MONEY RAISED FROM SELLING THE WOOL WAS DONATED TO THE RED CROSS. IF THESE SHEEP COULD TALK, WHAT DO YOU THINK THEY'D BE SAYING?

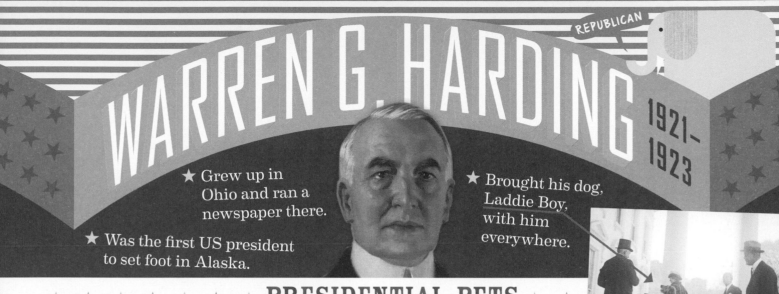

WARREN G. HARDING

REPUBLICAN

1921–1923

★ Grew up in Ohio and ran a newspaper there.

★ Was the first US president to set foot in Alaska.

★ Brought his dog, Laddie Boy, with him everywhere.

★ ★ ★ ★ ★ PRESIDENTIAL PETS ★ ★ ★

LADDIE BOY WAS SUCH A POPULAR PRESIDENTIAL PUP THAT A BRONZE STATUE WAS MADE OF HIM WHEN HE DIED. MANY PRESIDENTS HAD POPULAR PETS. CAN YOU MATCH THE PRESIDENT TO HIS ANIMAL COMPANION?

1 Thomas Jefferson		**A** Nanny and Nanko GOATS
2 Abraham Lincoln		**B** King Tut A BELGIAN SHEPHERD
3 William Henry Harrison		**C** Socks A CAT
4 Millard Fillmore		**D** Bo and Sunny PORTUGUESE WATER DOGS
5 Herbert Hoover		**E** Millie A GOLDEN SPRINGER SPANIEL
6 Dwight D. Eisenhower		**F** Liberty A GOLDEN RETRIEVER
7 Gerald Ford		**G** Gabby A PARAKEET
8 George H. W. Bush		**H** Sukey A COW
9 Bill Clinton		**I** Dick A MOCKINGBIRD
10 Barack Obama		**J** Mason and Dixon PONIES

CALVIN COOLIDGE

1923–1929

★ Called "Silent Cal" because he didn't talk much in public.

★ Lit the first national Christmas tree on the White House grounds.

★ First Lady Grace Coolidge was a teacher at a school for the deaf.

DECORATE THE WHITE HOUSE

OVER THE YEARS, MANY PRESIDENTS AND FIRST LADIES HAVE STARTED HOLIDAY TRADITIONS AT THE WHITE HOUSE. NOW IT'S YOUR CHANCE. DECORATE THE WHITE HOUSE ENTRANCE TO CELEBRATE YOUR FAVORITE HOLIDAY.

HERBERT HOOVER

REPUBLICAN

1929–1933

★ A self-made millionaire, he donated his presidential salary to charity.

★ Signed a law making "The Star-Spangled Banner" the national anthem.

★ Led the country at the start of the Great Depression.

★ ★ ★ ★ ★ ★ **O SAY CAN YOU SEE** ★ ★ ★ ★ ★ ★ ★

DRAW A PICTURE OF A PLACE IN YOUR COMMUNITY WHERE THE STAR-SPANGLED BANNER WAVES.

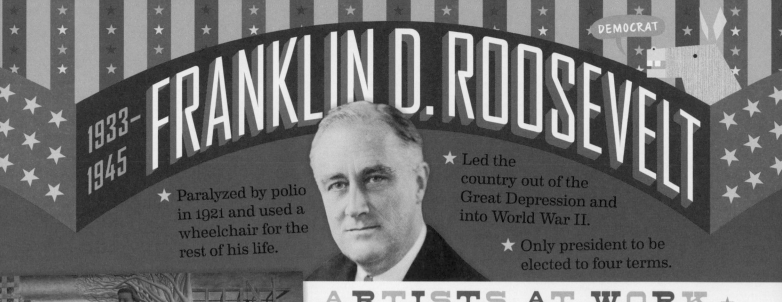

FRANKLIN D. ROOSEVELT

1933–1945

DEMOCRAT

★ Paralyzed by polio in 1921 and used a wheelchair for the rest of his life.

★ Led the country out of the Great Depression and into World War II.

★ Only president to be elected to four terms.

ARTISTS AT WORK ★

ROOSEVELT'S WORKS PROGRESS ADMINISTRATION HELPED KEEP ARTISTS, WRITERS, AND ACTORS EMPLOYED DURING THE DEPRESSION. THIS MURAL IN A GOVERNMENT BUILDING IN WASHINGTON, DC, WAS PAINTED BY A WPA ARTIST.

USE THE SPACE BELOW TO DESIGN A MURAL FOR A BUILDING WHERE YOU LIVE.

First Lady
ELEANOR ROOSEVELT
1933– 1945

★ First first lady to hold a press conference (1938); went on to hold 347 more.

★ Fought for the rights of women, African Americans, workers, and the poor.

★ Served as a US delegate to the United Nations.

★ ★ ★ ★ ★ FIRST LADY FACTS ★ ★ ★ ★ ★

UNSCRAMBLE THE WORDS TO FILL IN THESE FACTS ABOUT ELEANOR ROOSEVELT.

1 Eleanor Roosevelt was born in 1884 in WEN KROY City.

2 President Theodore Roosevelt was her CLUNE.

3 She was 5'1" tall, the same height as First Lady LEMHICEL Obama.

4 She married Franklin Roosevelt in 1905; they had six NERDLICH together.

5 As first lady, she wrote a RAPPEWENS column called My Day.

6 She once went on a nighttime flight with pilot AILMEA Earhart.

7 She served as chairman of the UN Commission of NAMUH Rights.

8 Before she became first lady, she worked as a CHERTEA.

9 During World War I and World War II, she DREETOLVUNE with the Red Cross.

10 She gave more than 1,400 PESSHCEE when she was first lady.

HARRY S TRUMAN

1945–1953

★ Made the first presidential speech on television in 1949.

★ Authorized the nuclear bombing of Japan during World War II.

★ Led the country during the Korean War.

★ ★ ★ ★ REACHING THE NATION ★ ★ ★ ★

TRUMAN GAVE HIS TELEVISION SPEECH FOR HIS 1949 INAUGURATION. HE ASKED AMERICANS TO CONSERVE FOOD TO HELP THE WORLD'S STARVING PEOPLE.

DRAW YOURSELF GIVING A PRESIDENTIAL SPEECH ON TV. WHAT WOULD YOUR SPEECH BE ABOUT?

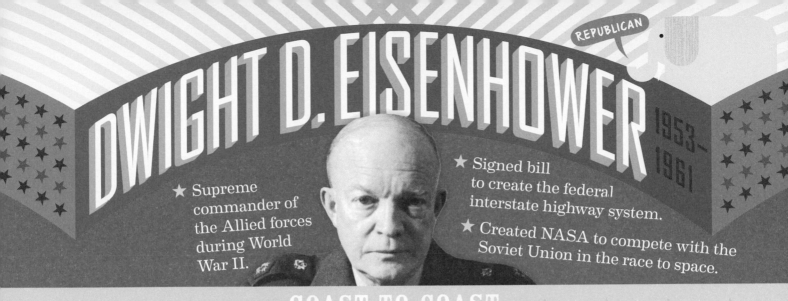

DWIGHT D. EISENHOWER

REPUBLICAN

1953–1961

★ Supreme commander of the Allied forces during World War II.

★ Signed bill to create the federal interstate highway system.

★ Created NASA to compete with the Soviet Union in the race to space.

★ COAST TO COAST ★

TODAY THE INTERSTATE HIGHWAY SYSTEM IS 46,876 MILES LONG AND CONNECTS MAJOR CITIES ACROSS THE CONTINENTAL UNITED STATES. TRACE A ROUTE FROM CALIFORNIA TO NEW YORK USING THE HIGHWAYS, VISITING AS MANY CITIES AS YOU CAN. CIRCLE THE NAMES OF CITIES YOU PASS THROUGH ON THE WAY.

SEATTLE, WASHINGTON

PORTLAND, OREGON

BILLINGS, MONTANA

BOISE, IDAHO

SALT LAKE CITY, UTAH

CHEYENNE, WYOMING

SAN FRANCISCO, CALIFORNIA

MINNEAPOLIS, MINNESOTA

PORTLAND, MAINE

BOSTON, MASSACHUSETTS

BUFFALO, NEW YORK

DETROIT, MICHIGAN

PHILADELPHIA, PENNSYLVANIA

NEW YORK, NEW YORK

DES MOINES, IOWA

CHICAGO, ILLINOIS

TOPEKA, KANSAS

INDIANAPOLIS, INDIANA

WASHINGTON, DC

RICHMOND, VIRGINIA

SANTA FE, NEW MEXICO

MEMPHIS, TENNESSEE

ATLANTA, GEORGIA

CHARLESTON, SOUTH CAROLINA

PHOENIX, ARIZONA

OKLAHOMA CITY, OKLAHOMA

DALLAS, TEXAS

MOBILE, ALABAMA

NEW ORLEANS, LOUISIANA

MIAMI, FLORIDA

ANCHORAGE, ALASKA

43

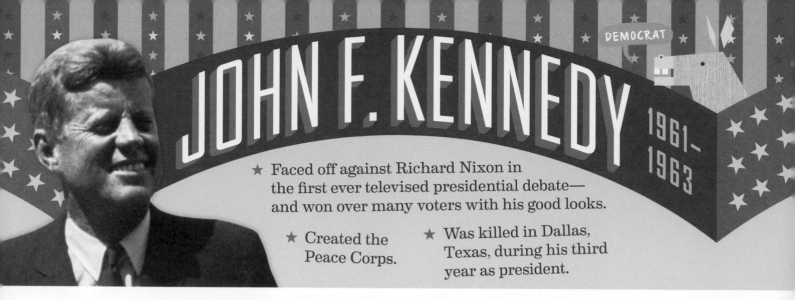

JOHN F. KENNEDY
1961–1963

DEMOCRAT

★ Faced off against Richard Nixon in the first ever televised presidential debate— and won over many voters with his good looks.

★ Created the Peace Corps.

★ Was killed in Dallas, Texas, during his third year as president.

★ ★ ★ ★ KENNEDY QUOTES ★ ★ ★ ★ ★

KENNEDY WAS KNOWN FOR HIS PASSIONATE SPEECHES. USE THE WORDS FROM THE WORD BANK TO FILL IN THESE FAMOUS QUOTES.

1 "Ask not what your country can do for you, ask what you can do for your ...."

2 "Those who look only to the past or .... are certain to miss the future."

3 "Forgive your ...., but never forget their names."

4 "If a society cannot help the many who are ....,
it cannot save the few who are rich."

5 "A man may die, nations may rise and fall, but an .... lives on."

6 "We choose to go to the .... in this decade and do other things, not because they are easy, but because they are ...."

7 "The cost of .... is always high, but Americans have always paid it."

8 "Things do not happen. Things are .... to happen."

9 "The best road to .... is freedom's road."

WORD BANK
country enemies freedom hard idea
made moon poor present progress

44

First Lady
JACQUELINE KENNEDY 1961–1963

★ Played an important role in restoring the White House and gave the first televised tour of the famous presidential home.

★ In support of civil rights, set up an integrated kindergarten in the White House for her daughter.

★ ★ ★ ★ ★ FIRST FASHIONS

IN ADDITION TO THE MANY THINGS SHE *DID*, FIRST LADY JACQUELINE KENNEDY WAS FAMOUS FOR WHAT SHE *WORE*.

DRAW WHAT YOU WOULD YOU WEAR TO A FANCY WHITE HOUSE EVENT.

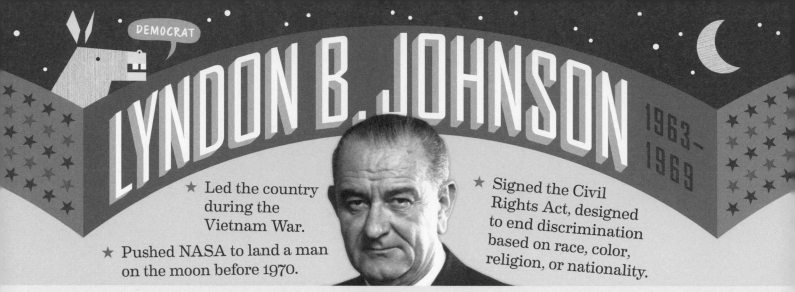

DEMOCRAT

LYNDON B. JOHNSON

1963–1969

★ Led the country during the Vietnam War.

★ Pushed NASA to land a man on the moon before 1970.

★ Signed the Civil Rights Act, designed to end discrimination based on race, color, religion, or nationality.

★ ★ ★ ★ ★ ★ ★ REACHING THE MOON ★ ★ ★ ★ ★ ★ ★

THE FIRST ASTRONAUTS WALKED ON THE MOON IN 1969, SHORTLY AFTER JOHNSON LEFT OFFICE. FILL IN THIS MOONSCAPE WITH SOMETHING YOU THINK THE ASTRONAUTS MIGHT HAVE BEEN SURPRISED TO SEE WHEN THEY LANDED.

RICHARD M. NIXON

REPUBLICAN

1969–1974

★ Restored US relations with China.

★ Started the Environmental Protection Agency.

★ First president to resign from office, for obstructing justice in the Watergate scandal.

★ ★ ★ ★ ★ **PANDA-MONIUM!** ★ ★ ★ ★ ★

IN 1972, CHINA SENT TWO GIANT PANDAS, HSING-HSING AND LING-LING, AS A GIFT TO PRESIDENT NIXON. IF THESE PANDAS COULD TALK, WHAT DO YOU THINK THEY'D BE SAYING?

GERALD R. FORD

1974–1977

★ Only president who was an Eagle Scout.

★ College-football star who could have played for the NFL.

★ Survived World War II, even after a typhoon hit his navy aircraft carrier.

★ Had an outdoor swimming pool and cabana installed at the White House.

PRESIDENTIAL FITNESS

GERALD FORD PRACTICED PHYSICAL FITNESS HIS WHOLE LIFE AND HOLDS THE RECORD FOR PRESIDENTIAL LONGEVITY. SHADE IN EACH BLOCK THAT CONTAINS AN X TO FIND OUT HOW MANY YEARS HE LIVED.

G	R	L	D	F	R	D	P	R	S	T
D	O	X	X	X	T	X	X	X	Y	L
P	X	O	Y	X	F	R	E	Q	X	T
R	X	A	N	X	Z	I	K	M	X	W
L	P	X	X	X	C	H	X	X	R	I
S	N	T	X	P	U	R	W	Q	X	C
B	L	X	V	F	O	M	M	P	X	R
K	X	B	V	N	W	X	X	X	P	O
K	R	A	B	N	R	F	G	T	K	M

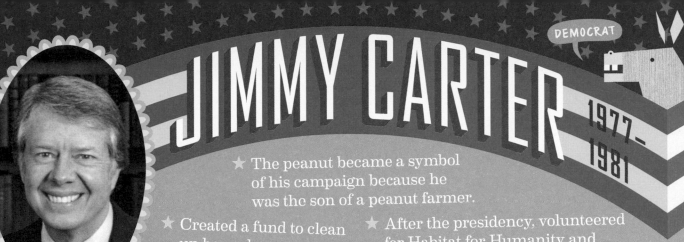

JIMMY CARTER

DEMOCRAT

1977–1981

★ The peanut became a symbol of his campaign because he was the son of a peanut farmer.

★ Created a fund to clean up hazardous waste dumps around the country.

★ After the presidency, volunteered for Habitat for Humanity and worked for peace in the Middle East.

★ FUTURE FOCUS ★

THIS PEANUT FLOAT HELPED CARTER CELEBRATE HIS INAUGURATION. AT AN INAUGURATION, A PRESIDENT USUALLY GIVES A SPEECH ABOUT HIS PLANS AND HOPES FOR THE COUNTRY'S FUTURE. WHAT FIVE THINGS WOULD YOU PROMISE THE NATION IN *YOUR* INAUGURATION SPEECH?

❶

❷

❸

❹

❺

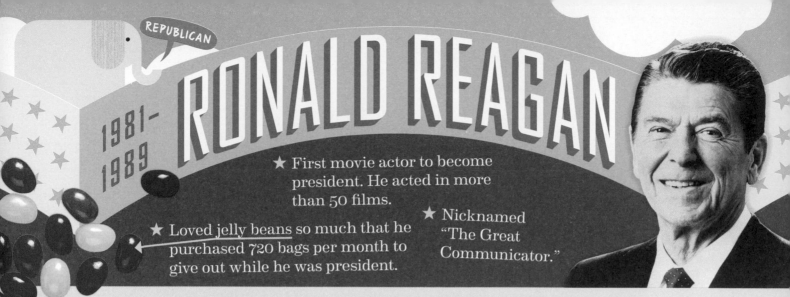

RONALD REAGAN

1981–1989

★ First movie actor to become president. He acted in more than 50 films.

★ Loved jelly beans so much that he purchased 720 bags per month to give out while he was president.

★ Nicknamed "The Great Communicator."

★ ★ ★ NOW BOARDING ★ ★ ★ ★

RONALD REAGAN WASHINGTON NATIONAL AIRPORT IS NAMED AFTER THE FORTIETH PRESIDENT. HE FLEW ON AIR FORCE ONE, THE PRESIDENT'S OFFICIAL PLANE, BUT AS A TRAVELER TO WASHINGTON, DC, YOU'D HAVE TO GET THROUGH THIS AIRPORT MAZE TO GET TO YOUR BOARDING GATE. GO!

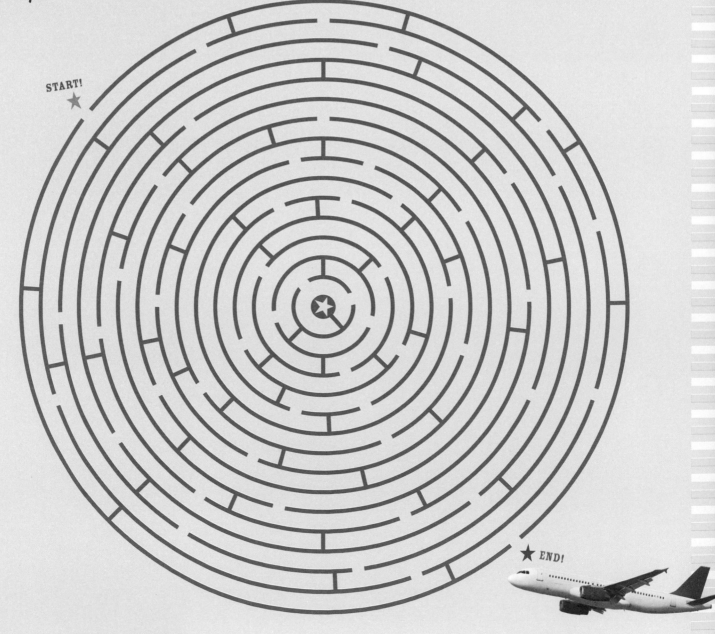

START!

★ END!

GEORGE H. W. BUSH
1989–1993

★ Flew combat missions in World War II.

★ Led the country during the Persian Gulf War.

★ Hated broccoli so much that he banned it from Air Force One.

★ ★ ★ ★ ★ ★ ★ ★ ★ **FRIES IN THE SKY** ★ ★ ★ ★ ★ ★ ★ ★

PRESIDENTS SPEND A LOT OF TIME TRAVELING ALL OVER THE NATION AND THE WORLD; AIR FORCE ONE GETS THEM THERE. CHEFS ON THE GROUND AND IN THE AIR MAKE THE PRESIDENT'S FAVORITE FOODS—EVERYTHING FROM BURGERS TO LASAGNA.

WHAT WOULD YOUR MENU LOOK LIKE IF YOU WERE PRESIDENT?

AIR FORCE ONE

Breakfast

Lunch

Dinner

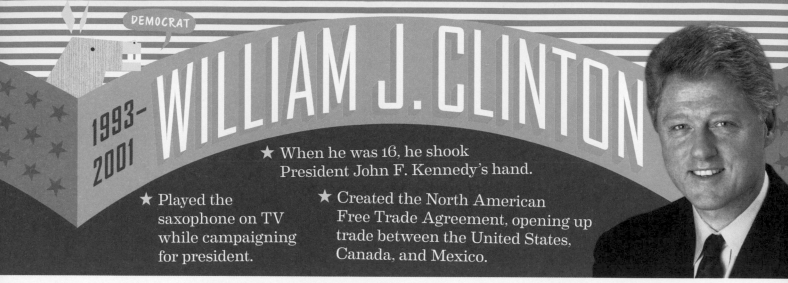

DEMOCRAT

1993–2001

WILLIAM J. CLINTON

★ When he was 16, he shook President John F. Kennedy's hand.

★ Played the saxophone on TV while campaigning for president.

★ Created the North American Free Trade Agreement, opening up trade between the United States, Canada, and Mexico.

★ ★ ★ ★ ★ FROM GOVERNOR TO PRESIDENT ★ ★ ★ ★ ★

BILL CLINTON WAS GOVERNOR OF ARKANSAS BEFORE HE BECAME PRESIDENT. THE PRESIDENTS ON THIS LIST SERVED AS GOVERNORS, TOO. CAN YOU MATCH THEM TO THEIR STATES?

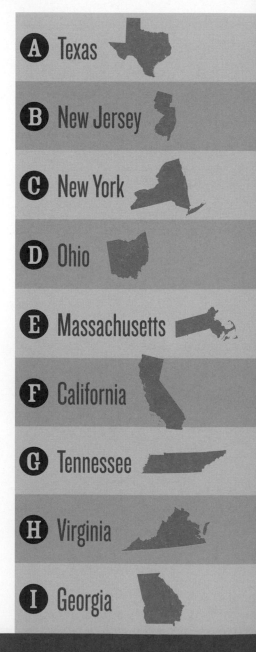

Thomas Jefferson

Jimmy Carter

Andrew Johnson

George W. Bush

Grover Cleveland

Woodrow Wilson

Rutherford B. Hayes

Ronald Reagan

Calvin Coolidge

A Texas

B New Jersey

C New York

D Ohio

E Massachusetts

F California

G Tennessee

H Virginia

I Georgia

First Lady
HILLARY CLINTON ★ 1993–2001

★ First first lady to become a senator.

★ First first lady to become secretary of state.

★ First first lady to run for president.

★ ★ ★ ★ ★ ★ ★ **FIRST LADY FIRSTS** ★ ★

CAN YOU MATCH EACH FIRST LADY TO HER ACCOMPLISHMENT? (HINT: LOOK AT THE YEARS EACH FIRST LADY SERVED.)

1 Martha Washington
1789–1797

2 Abigail Adams
1797–1801

3 Julia Tyler
1841–1845

4 Abigail Fillmore
1850–1853

5 Mary Todd Lincoln
1861–1865

6 Lucy Hayes
1877–1881

7 Caroline Harrison
1889–1893

8 Florence Harding
1921–1923

9 Pat Nixon
1969–1974

10 Rosalynn Carter
1977–1981

A First to hold a séance in the White House.

B First to vote.

C First to host an Easter Egg Roll on the White House lawn.

D First to be mother of a president.

E First to wear pants in public.

F First to be on a postage stamp.

G First to have a job before marrying.

H First to use electricity.

I First to have a VCR in the White House.

J First to be photographed.

53

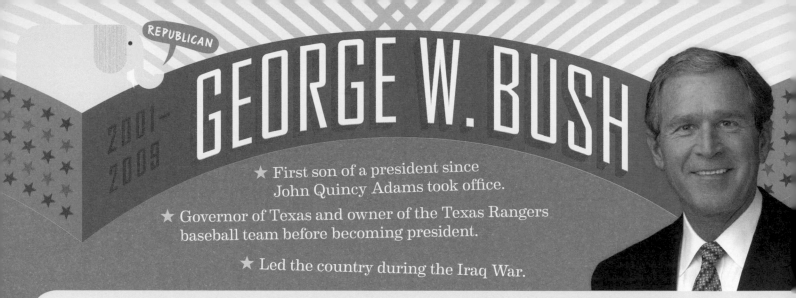

GEORGE W. BUSH

2001–2009

★ First son of a president since John Quincy Adams took office.

★ Governor of Texas and owner of the Texas Rangers baseball team before becoming president.

★ Led the country during the Iraq War.

★ ★ ★ LITTLE RANCH ON THE PRAIRIE ★ ★ ★

PRESIDENT BUSH AND FIRST LADY LAURA BUSH SPENT TIME DURING THE PRESIDENCY ON THEIR 1,600-ACRE RANCH IN TEXAS PRAIRIE COUNTRY. THE TEXAS PRAIRIE IS HOME TO MANY ANIMALS, INCLUDING THE ARMADILLO, PRAIRIE DOG, MOCKINGBIRD, AND TEXAS RAT SNAKE.
DRAW SOME PRAIRIE ANIMALS INTO THIS RANCH.

First Lady
LAURA BUSH
2001–2009

★ Worked as a second-grade teacher and librarian.

★ Worked to improve literacy and education.

★ Started a National Book Festival in Washington, DC.

★ ★

FIRST LADY LAURA BUSH OVERSAW RENOVATIONS OF THE WHITE HOUSE LIBRARY. HOW WOULD YOU DESIGN YOUR VERY OWN LIBRARY OR READING ROOM?

BARACK OBAMA

2009– 2017

★ First African American to hold the office of US president.

★ Won the 2009 Nobel Peace Prize for working for cooperation between the nations of the world.

★ Had the White House tennis court adapted so he could play basketball on it.

HAWAII

★ ALOHA! ★

HAWAII BECAME A STATE IN 1959, WHEN DWIGHT D. EISENHOWER WAS PRESIDENT. TWO YEARS LATER, BARACK OBAMA WAS BORN THERE. THE ISLAND STATE IS HOME TO MANY BEAUTIFUL FLOWERS AND BIRDS. LOOK AT THE LIST. CAN YOU GUESS WHICH IS WHICH? CIRCLE YOUR ANSWER.

Oleander   IS IT A 🌸 OR A 🐦 ?

Saffron Finch   IS IT A 🌸 OR A 🐦 ?

Cinnamon Teal   IS IT A 🌸 OR A 🐦 ?

Gardenia   IS IT A 🌸 OR A 🐦 ?

5 Nutmeg Mannikin   IS IT A 🌸 OR A 🐦 ?

6 Plumeria   IS IT A 🌸 OR A 🐦 ?

7 Zebra Dove   IS IT A 🌸 OR A 🐦 ?

8 White Pikake   IS IT A 🌸 OR A 🐦 ?

9 Pacific Golden Plover   IS IT A 🌸 OR A 🐦 ?

First Lady
MICHELLE OBAMA

2009–2017

★ Worked to help military families.

★ Launched Let's Move!, a kids' health program.

★ First African American first lady.

★ With students, planted a vegetable garden on the White House South Lawn.

★ ★ ★ ★ ★ **LET YOUR GARDEN GROW** ★ ★ ★ ★ ★

BROCCOLI, SPINACH, AND RADISHES ARE SOME OF THE VEGETABLES GROWN IN THE WHITE HOUSE VEGETABLE GARDEN. FILL THIS GARDEN SPACE WITH YOUR FAVORITE VEGGIES.

VOTE!

THROUGHOUT AMERICAN HISTORY, MANY PEOPLE HAVE FOUGHT HARD FOR EQUAL RIGHTS IN VOTING. BUT IN THE 2012 PRESIDENTIAL ELECTION, ONLY 54.7% OF AMERICAN CITIZENS ELIGIBLE TO VOTE ACTUALLY VOTED!

CREATE A "GET OUT THE VOTE" POSTER. THEN HANG IT UP WHERE ADULTS YOU KNOW CAN SEE IT WHENEVER THERE'S AN ELECTION!

You, the President!

IT'S THE YEAR 2052, AND YOU'VE TAKEN OFFICE AS PRESIDENT OF THE UNITED STATES! DRAW YOUR OFFICIAL PORTRAIT HERE.

Fun Facts ABOUT THE White House

- ★ George Washington chose the site for the White House in 1791.

- ★ The White House was known as the Executive Mansion, the President's House, or the President's Palace until Theodore Roosevelt made its current name official in 1901.

- ★ How much paint does it take to make the White House white? 570 gallons!

- ★ During the War of 1812, British troops stormed the White House. President James Madison and his wife, Dolley, had already fled. The soldiers ate a meal and then set the White House on fire.

- ★ In August 1924, some visitors and residents, including First Lady Grace Coolidge and Prime Minister Winston Churchill, claim they saw the ghost of Abraham Lincoln in the White House.

★ ★ FUN ON THE SOUTH LAWN ★ ★

EVERY YEAR, THE WHITE HOUSE HOSTS AN EASTER EGG ROLL ON THE SOUTH LAWN. IN PAST YEARS, THERE HAVE ALSO BEEN MAYPOLE DANCERS, BROADWAY PERFORMERS, AN ANTIQUES CAR SHOW, AND A PETTING ZOO ON THE LAWN.

WHAT KIND OF FUN EVENT WOULD YOU THROW ON THE SOUTH LAWN IF YOU WERE PRESIDENT? DRAW IT HERE.

★ WHITE HOUSE BY THE NUMBERS ★

412	**132**	**35**	**28**	**3**
doors	rooms	bathrooms	fireplaces	elevators

ANSWERS

PAGE 4

```
          M A R T H A
              W I G
          W   I C
        D   I
      M O U N T V E R N O N
      O   R   R
      L   T   G
      L   H   I
    T E E T   N   I N D I A N
      A       I
      R       A
  C H E R R Y
```

PAGE 8

PAGE 10

1 LOUISIANA
2 MISSOURI
3 ARKANSAS
4 IOWA
5 NORTH DAKOTA
6 SOUTH DAKOTA
7 NEBRASKA
8 OKLAHOMA
9 KANSAS
10 COLORADO
11 WYOMING
12 MONTANA
13 MINNESOTA

PAGE 15

```
L A C H L A N O Y L
E N N A L I L T J O
J O H N L L M D O N
M R L H L U A D H T
A P E C E J R I N T
L E T H W L Y V J R
I A I I E F Y A R E
C R C O Z H N D R B
E L I Z A B E T H O
T Y A F T R E B O R
```

PAGE 16

1 MYSTERY
2 JAPAN
3 TREE HOUSE
4 SOLDIER
5 TELEVISION
6 NURSE
7 FIGHTER
8 CONGRESS
9 SENIOR PROM
10 BALLET

PAGE 18

1 IOWA
2 OREGON
3 TEXAS
4 CALIFORNIA
5 UTAH
6 WISCONSIN
7 MONTANA
8 WASHINGTON
9 IDAHO
10 NEW MEXICO
11 COLORADO
12 ARIZONA
13 NEVADA

PAGE 22

VIRGINIA
TENNESSEE
NORTH CAROLINA
ARKANSAS
SOUTH CAROLINA
GEORGIA
TEXAS
LOUISIANA
ALABAMA
FLORIDA
MISSISSIPPI

PAGE 24

```
L     C A T
A     A T A L
W R E S T L I N G
Y       L       M
E       E       A
B E A R D       R
R       K E N T U C K Y
```

PAGE 25

```
M U S K O X A L P A S
S O X K W H A L E A A
A B O L A A S E E X P
L I F S K R A L H O O
M R D A E B T G S F L
O A E L A O S A L C A
N C R K M R L E L I R
A A L R A S Y D A T B
G O A T S E N L D C E
K M I N K A X A A R A
G R I Z Z L Y B E A R
```

PAGE 27

1873: BLUE JEANS
1876: TELEPHONE
1877: PHONOGRAPH
1879: LIGHTBULB
1882: ELECTRIC FAN
1884: ROLLER COASTER
1891: ESCALATOR
1892: AUTOMOBILE
1893: ZIPPER

PAGE 31

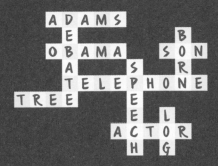

ADAMS
OBAMA SON
TELEPHONE
TREE
ACTOR

PAGE 33

PAGE 37

1. Jefferson .... I. Dick
2. Lincoln .... A. Nanny and Nanko
3. Harrison .... H. Sukey
4. Fillmore .... J. Mason and Dixon
5. Hoover .... B. King Tut
6. Eisenhower .... G. Gabby
7. Ford .... F. Liberty
8. Bush .... E. Millie
9. Clinton .... C. Socks
10. Obama .... D. Bo and Sunny

PAGE 41

1. NEW YORK
2. UNCLE
3. MICHELLE
4. CHILDREN
5. NEWSPAPER

6. AMELIA
7. HUMAN
8. TEACHER
9. VOLUNTEERED
10. SPEECHES

PAGE 44

1. COUNTRY
2. PRESENT
3. ENEMIES
4. POOR
5. IDEA
6. MOON HARD
7. FREEDOM
8. MADE
9. PROGRESS

PAGE 48

PAGE 50

PAGE 52

1. Jefferson .... H. Virginia
2. Carter .... I. Georgia

3. Johnson .... G. Tennessee
4. Bush .... A. Texas
5. Cleveland .... C. New York
6. Wilson .... B. New Jersey
7. Hayes .... D. Ohio
8. Reagan .... F. California
9. Coolidge .... E. Massachusetts

PAGE 53

1. Martha Washington — F. First to be on a postage stamp.
2. Abigail Adams — D. First to be mother of a president.
3. Julia Tyler — J. First to be photographed.
4. Abigail Fillmore — G. First to have a job before marrying.
5. Mary Todd Lincoln — A. First to hold a séance in the White House.
6. Lucy Hayes — C. First to host an Easter Egg Roll on the White House lawn.
7. Caroline Harrison — H. First to use electricity.
8. Florence Harding — B. First to vote.
9. Pat Nixon — E. First to wear pants in public.
10. Rosalynn Carter — I. First to have a VCR in the White House.

PAGE 56

1. OLEANDER
2. SAFFRON FINCH
3. CINNAMON TEAL
4. GARDENIA
5. NUTMEG MANNIKIN
6. PLUMERIA
7. ZEBRA DOVE
8. WHITE PIKAKE
9. PACIFIC GOLDEN PLOVER

PHOTO CREDITS

MAKE YOUR OWN OVAL OFFICE

★ DECORATE IN YOUR FAVORITE COLORS.

★ DRAW PICTURES YOU LIKE IN THE FRAMES.

★ DESIGN YOUR OWN PRESIDENTIAL RUG.

★ THEN PUNCH OUT ALONG THE LINES, GLUE THE TABS TOGETHER, AND YOU'VE GOT YOUR OWN OVAL OFFICE. HAIL TO THE CHIEF!

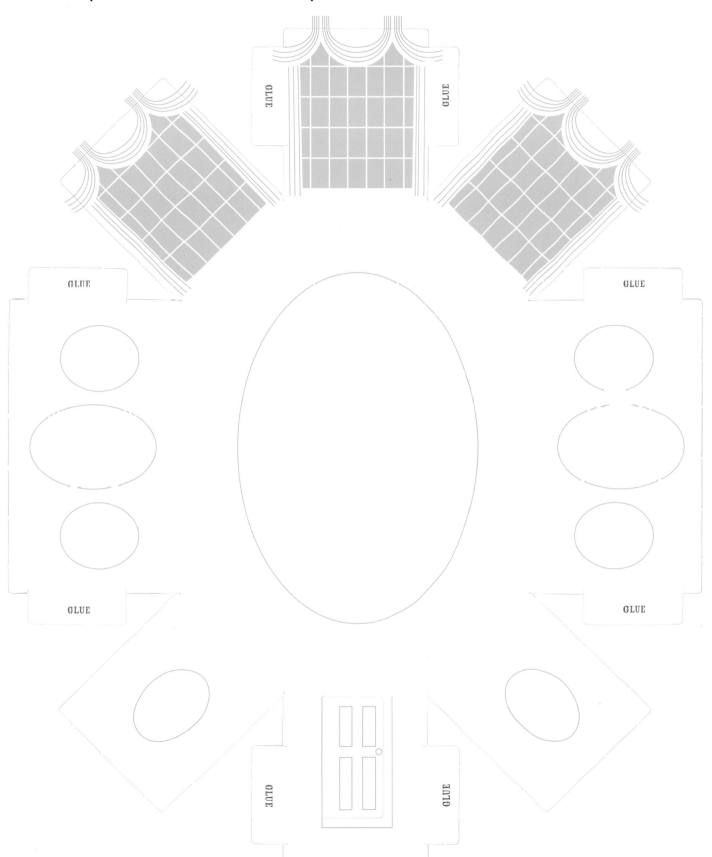